Why the Chimes Rang: A Play in One Act

Elizabeth Apthorp McFadden

Contents

PREFACE. 7
WHY THE CHIMES RANG. 9
CHARACTERS. 9
APPENDIX. 31
SCENERY. 32
LIGHTING. 36
MUSIC. 38
COSTUMES. 42
PROPERTIES. 45

WHY THE CHIMES RANG: A PLAY IN ONE ACT

BY

Elizabeth Apthorp McFadden

PREFACE.

This little play is prentice work done in Professor George P. Baker's class, English 47 at Radcliffe College in the fall of 1908. Several years later it was staged by Professor Baker in the "47 Workshop," his laboratory for trying out plays written in the Harvard and Radcliffe courses in dramatic technique.

I am glad to acknowledge here my indebtedness to the "Shop" and its workers for this chance of seeing the play in action. Of the various advantages which a "Workshop" performance secures to the author none is more helpful than the mass of written criticism handed in by the audience, and representing some two or three hundred frank and widely varying views of the work in question. I am especially grateful for this constructive criticism, much of which has been of real service in the subsequent rewriting of the piece.

"Why the Chimes Rang" was again tried out the next year in seven performances by the "Workshop" company in various Boston settlements. Other groups of amateurs have given it in Arlington, Massachusetts, Los Angeles, California and in Honolulu. These performances have proved that while its setting may seem to call for the equipment of a theatre, the play can be acceptably given in any hall or Sunday school room.

Suggestions for the simplest possible staging have been added to the present publication in an appendix which contains data on the scenery, music, lighting, costumes and properties for the piece.

ELIZABETH APTHORP McFADDEN.

WHY THE CHIMES RANG.

CHARACTERS.

HOLGER......................*A peasant boy*
STEEN......................*His younger brother*
BERTEL.....................*Their uncle*
AN OLD WOMAN
LORDS, LADIES, *etc.*--

TIME:--*Dusk of a day of long ago*.

* * * * *

SCENE:-- *The interior of a wood-chopper's hut on the edge of a forest*.

Why the Chimes Rang.

The scene is laid in a peasant's hut on the edge of a forest near a cathedral town. It is a dark low-raftered room lit only by the glowing wood fire in the great fireplace in the wall to the right, and by a faint moonlight that steals in through the little window high in the left wall. This window commands a view of the cathedral and of the road leading down into the town. The only entrance into the hut is the front door near the window.

The furnishings are few: two substantial stools, one near the window, the other before the fire, logs piled up near the hearth, and on the chimney shelf above a few dishes, three little bowls, three spoons and a great iron porridge pot. A wooden peg to the right of the chimney holds Steen's cap and cape, one to the left an old shawl. Near the door Holger's cap and cape hang from a third peg.

Despite its poverty the room is full of beautiful coloring as it lies half hidden in deep shadow save where the light of the fire falls on the brown of the wood and the warmer shades of the children's garments, illuminates their faces and gleams on their bright hair.

When the curtain is raised Steen is sitting disconsolately on the stool near the fire. He is a handsome sturdy little lad of nine or ten, dressed in rough but warm garments of a dark red. Holger a slender boy some four years older, bends over Steen patting him comfortingly on the shoulder.

There is petulance and revolt in the expression of the younger boy but Holger's face is full of a blended character and spirituality that makes him beautiful. He is clad like his brother in comfortable but worn jerkin and hose of a dark leaf green. His manner to the little boy is full of affection, though occasionally he is superior after the manner of big brothers. Throughout the play, two moods alternate in Holger, a certain grave, half-mystical dreaminess and bubbling through it, the high spirits of his natural boyish self.

HOLGER. Take heart, Steen, perhaps we can go next year.

STEEN. Next year! Next year I'll be so old I won't want to go.

HOLGER. Oh, quite old folks go to the Christmas service. Come, let's watch the people going down to town.

STEEN. No.

HOLGER. The road'll be full, grand folk! (*He crosses to the window*) Come watch, Steen.

STEEN. No!

HOLGER. (*Looking out*) Why the road's all empty again!

STEEN. (*In a wailing tone*) Everybody's gone!

HOLGER. (*Trying to be brave*) They're lighting the cathedral!

STEEN. I don't care!

HOLGER. Oh, Steen, come see,--like the stars coming out!

STEEN. I won't see! Mother said way last summer that we could go to-night, and now--(*His voice breaks in a sob*)

HOLGER. She meant it! She didn't know that the grandmother would be ill, and she and father'ud have to go to *her*. Be fair, Steen!

STEEN. They might let us go alone. "Too little!" Bah!

HOLGER. (*In a low almost frightened tone*) Steen, come here!

(*The tone, rather than the words, take* STEEN *quickly to* HOLGER'S *side*.)

STEEN. What?

HOLGER. (*Pointing out the window*) Look, by the dead pine yonder, an old woman facing us, kneeling in the snow, see? praying!

STEEN. (*In an awed tone*) She's looking at us!

HOLGER. She's raising her hand to us!

STEEN. She's beckoning!

HOLGER. No, she's making the Sign of the Cross.

(*Both boys drop their heads devoutly.*)

STEEN. Who is she, Holger?

HOLGER. I don't know.

STEEN. (*Drawing back from the window and crossing the room to the fire*) Oh, Holger, I'm afraid!

HOLGER. No, no! Look, she has turned away,--she's deeper in the shadow,--why, she's gone! (*Following* STEEN *with all his bright courage bubbling high again, and speaks in a bantering tone*) Just some old granny going down to town, and thou afraid!

STEEN. (*Recovering also*) And *thou* afraid!

HOLGER. I was not!

STEEN. (*Derisively*) Oh-h-h-h!

HOLGER. Well, I was just a little bit afraid--lest she might frighten thee. (*Steps are heard outside the house. Both boys start and look frightened again*) Hush,--steps--coming here!

STEEN. (*Backing from the door*) The old woman!

HOLGER. (*Crosses the room, looks cautiously out of the window, then cries joyously*) No,--Uncle Bertel!

BERTEL. (*Off stage*) Hullo, there,--open, Holger!

> (STEEN *and* HOLGER *make a dash for the door, fling it open and* BERTEL *enters. He is a jolly robust peasant uncle of early middle life, clad in rough gray jerkin and hose, with a dark gray cloak wrapped about him. He so radiates cheer that the room seems warmer for his presence in it. Nothing to be afraid of about him, the children adore him.*)

STEEN. (*Clinging to him, happily*) Oh, Uncle, Uncle, Uncle Bertel!

HOLGER. (*Seizing* BERTEL *on his other side*) Uncle Bertel, welcome!

BERTEL. (*Tousling their hair and shaking himself loose in pretended dismay*) Help, help!--Robbers!--I'm beset!--Gently, youngsters!--(***He goes over to the fire and stands warming himself***) Brrrrr! It's cold in the forest to-night!--Well, (***He faces them genially***) why am I come?--Tell me that!

STEEN. (***Exultantly***) To take us to the Christmas Service?

HOLGER. Uncle! How didst thou know we were not going?

BERTEL. I met a fox--who said--

HOLGER. Oh-h!--Thou hast seen mother and father!

BERTEL. (***Draws the stool nearer the fire and sits, the children promptly drop on the floor beside him***) By our Lady, yes!--and walking so fast they had only time to throw me a word from the sides of their mouths. "Go up," cried Mother,--"I wist my boys are deep in tears!"--and I, not wishing to see you drown in so much water--

HOLGER. (***Patting his arm***) Dear Uncle Bertel!

STEEN. (***Rising on his knees***) Come, let's go quick!

BERTEL. Patience, patience, young colt, plenty of time, mother said something else.

STEEN. What?

BERTEL. (***His eye on the shelf above the fire***) That I should find some warm porridge for my pains.

HOLGER. (***Springing to his feet***) Why, of course, there *is* porridge! (***He goes to the shelf***) Nice and warm it is! All ready for supper. (***He hands the first bowl to*** BERTEL, STEEN ***capers nimbly across the intervening space and seats himself on the side of the hearth, facing*** BERTEL, ***his back to the audience***)

STEEN. Supper! How could we forget supper?--Give me a ***big*** bowlful, Holger.

HOLGER. (***Handing*** STEEN ***his porridge***) There isn't a ***big*** bowlful here.

STEEN. (***Taking the bowl and hugging it***) Nice kind good supper, umh! (***Begins to eat eagerly***)

HOLGER. (***Suddenly looking toward the door***) Listen!

BERTEL. To what?

HOLGER. (***Awed, hesitant***) Someone--sobbing--at the door! (***He goes to it, the others watching him startled, he opens the door, finds nothing, closes it and comes back***) Nothing there!

BERTEL. The wind!--Thy old tricks, Holger,--always dreaming some strange thing.

HOLGER. (***Recalled by*** BERTEL'S ***words to something else***) Didst thou pass an old woman on the road--near here?

BERTEL. Not a soul nearer than the town gate. (HOLGER ***stands thinking, absorbed***) Come, boy, eat,--***eat***! See how Steen eats!

HOLGER. (***Breaks through his abstraction and reverts to his bright*** *self)* Oh, Uncle Bertel,--I'm too glad to eat!

BERTEL. (*More seriously*) Thou art right, lad,--fasting were better than feasting this day in Tralsund!--they say,--do you know what they say in the town?

HOLGER. What?

BERTEL. They say--that to-night in the great church--when the offerings are laid upon the altar for the Christ child,--***something will happen***!

> (STEEN has finished his porridge, puts the bowl on the shelf near him, seizes his cloak and cap from the peg near the hearth and stands eager to be gone.)

HOLGER. What?

BERTEL. Who can say? All day the folk have been pouring into the town as never before. The market place is crowded, every inn is full. No church but the cathedral could hold such a multitude. Never have I seen such excitement, such fervor!

HOLGER. There will be many gifts!

BERTEL. --the rich are bringing their treasure, gold and jewels, king's ransoms, aye and the King comes. (BERTEL *finishes his porridge and hands the bowl to* STEEN)

HOLGER. The King?

BERTEL. The King Himself!

STEEN. Oh, and shall we see Him, Uncle, and the fine gifts and everything?

BERTEL. Why not?--Even the poorest may go up and give--what hast thou to offer?

STEEN. (*Abashed*) I?--Nothing! (***Puts his porridge bowl and*** BERTEL'S ***on the shelf then goes restlessly to the door***)

HOLGER. (***Breaking in with eagerness***) Oh, I have, see, Uncle? (***Feels in his pocket and brings out two pennies***) See!--Last week I was gathering sticks in the forest and a fine gentleman rode past and asked the way of me. I showed him the path and he gave me these! (***Holds up the pennies***)

BERTEL. (***Rising and going to*** HOLGER ***who is in the middle of the room***) Faith, real money in the family. (***Stoops and looks at the pennies as though they were a rare sight***)

STEEN. Oh, I thought we were going to buy cakes with those, Holger.

HOLGER. But it's better to give it to the Christ Child. You see He is a little child, smaller than even you,--and I think He would like a little gift,--a little bright gift that would buy cakes for Him. (HOLGER ***goes toward the window and stands looking dreamily out at the lights of the church***)

BERTEL. Aye, to-night we must think of Him,--there in His Holy Church.

HOLGER. It *is* a holy place, the church!--I feel it every time I go,--it's like God's forest,--the pillars like old oaks and the great windows all colors like sunsets through the trees.

BERTEL. *'Tis* like the forest.

HOLGER. And when the organ plays that's like a storm gathering in the mountains.

BERTEL. A storm?--Aye!--"The Lord hath His way in the whirlwind and in the storm and the clouds are the dust of His feet!"--Why should He not do a wonder as of old? Perhaps the great miracle will come again!

HOLGER. Oh, which, Uncle?--There are so many in the Bible!

STEEN. Yes, which?--Would there be a whale now to swallow a priest?

BERTEL. Thou goosey! This was no Bible miracle,--it happened there, *there*, where we see the lights,--hundreds of years ago. (BERTEL *has followed* HOLGER *to the window and* STEEN *joins them. As he speaks* BERTEL *slips his arms affectionately round both children and the three stand looking out. At this moment something stirs in the dim shadows that shroud the corner up above the fire-place. Suddenly out of the dark the* OLD WOMAN *emerges. A tall figure, if she were not so bent, wrapped in a black cloak. There is nothing grotesque or sinister in her appearance, she might have stood for a statue of old age, impressive in its pathos. As she sits on the stool near the fire she throws back the cloak disclosing the plain straight dress of gray beneath. The light of the fire reveals her crouched, swaying back and forth praying silently, her face still shaded by the heavy hood of her cloak. The others gazing intently out at the church do not see her.* BERTEL *continues speaking*) Surely thou hast heard of the Miracle of the Chimes?

HOLGER. I've heard folks speak of it,--but I never knew just what happened.

STEEN. Oh, tell us, Uncle Bertel.

BERTEL. Aye, listen then!--You see the great tower there?--(***Both children nod emphatically***) It goes so high into the clouds that no one can see it's top!--No one even knows how high it is for the men who built it have been dead for hundreds of years.

STEEN. But what has that to do with the chimes?

HOLGER. Hush, Steen, let uncle speak!

BERTEL. The chimes are up at the top of the tower--and they are holy bells,--miraculous bells, placed there by sainted hands,--and when they rang 'twas said that angels' voices echoed through them.

STEEN. Why doesn't someone ring them *now*?

BERTEL. Ah, that is not so easy!--They are said to ring on Christmas Eve when the gifts are laid on the altar for the Christ-child,--but not every offering will ring them, it must be a perfect gift. And for all these years not one thing has been laid upon the altar good enough to make the chimes ring out.

HOLGER. Oh, that's what the priest was talking about to mother, then. He said it mustn't be just a fine gift for show but something full of love for the Christ-child.

STEEN. Oh, I want to hear them!

BERTEL. **We shall!**--The very air is full of holy mystery! The Spirit of Christ will be there in the church to-night! (***To*** HOLGER) Thy cap, boy!

(HOLGER *stands wrapt in thought gazing out at the cathedral.*)

STEEN. (*Taking the cap and cloak from the peg near the door and bringing them down and piling them into* HOLGER'S *arms*) Here they are, old dreamer!--(*He turns back up toward the door in such a way that he does not see the silent figure in the corner*) And hurry!

(BERTEL *too turns toward his left hand and does not see the woman.*)

HOLGER. (*In a tone of bright happiness, roused from his dreaming*) I'm coming!--Nothing can happen to stop us now, can it? (*As he says this he wheels to his right in a way that brings the chimney corner in his line of vision. He starts, bends forward staring as the others open the door, then he speaks in a tone that is little more than a gasp*) Steen!

(The others stop and stare at him, then in the direction of his look.)

STEEN. Oh!--The Old Woman!

BERTEL. (*Looking to* STEEN) When did she come in?

STEEN. I didn't see her!

(HOLGER *crosses timidly towards her. As he approaches the* OLD WOMAN *turns her eyes on him and holds out her hands in pitiful appeal.*)

HOLGER. What dost thou want, dame?

OLD WOMAN. (*In a voice that is harsh and broken*) Refuge--from the storm of the world!

HOLGER. Surely thou shalt rest here.

OLD WOMAN. (*Half rises stiffly as* HOLGER *draws nearer*) Oh, son, I am so weary and so heavy laden. (*She sways and* HOLGER *runs forward, catching her in his arms and supporting her on the stool. The others stand watching. She sits huddled forward in a position that suggests collapse*)

HOLGER. She's faint! (*He touches her hands*) She's so cold! Quick, Steen, build up the fire! (STEEN *goes to the fire and puts on another log, the flames blaze up.* HOLGER *busies himself chafing the woman's hands and covering her with the old cloak that has dropped back from her shoulders*) She must have lost her way in the forest.

BERTEL. (*Stands watching the woman rather suspiciously, now comes to* HOLGER *taps him on the arm and draws him a little apart, speaking in an undertone*) We have scant time to lose with that old beggar.

HOLGER. What'll I do with her?

BERTEL. Leave her and come on.

STEEN. And *come*--before it is to-morrow! (*He is back by the door, his hand on the latch*)

HOLGER. (*Turns and looks at the old woman and then back to* BERTEL) Oh, I--ought we to go and leave her?

STEEN. Not go?

BERTEL. Go, of course we'll go, she'll warm herself and march along.

HOLGER. But she is ill. (*Turns to* STEEN **with new decision in his manner**) Thou shalt go with Uncle but I--must stay with her.

BERTEL. Nonsense, Holger!

HOLGER. No, it isn't!--If we should all go now, the fire would go out and the light,--and she would wake up in the cold darkness and not know where to turn for help.

BERTEL. Na, by Saint Christopher!--Miss a miracle to keep company with a beggar!--Who held her hand before thou camest along? Send her packing and make haste, Holger.

STEEN. Oh, do, Holger!

HOLGER. If there were some place near that we could take her.

BERTEL. There isn't a place on the road,--they've all gone to town long ago. Bid her fare there also!

HOLGER. (**Looks at the** OLD WOMAN, **then at** BERTEL, **then back to the** OLD WOMAN, **then he shakes his head**) Mother wouldn't treat her so,--she'd be good to her.

BERTEL. Think of what you'll miss! (***An expression of anguish passes over*** HOLGER'S ***face, but he shakes his head and turns toward the old woman***) Well, this is idle talk, thou and I will go, Steen.

STEEN. Oh, come,--let's go!

Why the Chimes Rang: A Play in One Act

BERTEL. (*To* STEEN, *but for* HOLGER'S *benefit*) Thou and I will see the King, perchance--The Christ! Thou art stubborn, Holger, I who am older tell thee what to do! (HOLGER *shakes his head again*) Come, Steen! (*He opens the door and goes out*)

STEEN. (*Following him*) Good-bye, Holger.

HOLGER. Good-bye! (STEEN *goes out and shuts the door. There is a moment's pause while* HOLGER *stands staring at the closed door, then he suddenly runs toward it*) Oh, wait, wait for me, Uncle, I will go! (*He opens the door, starts to go through it, then stops, turns and looks at the Woman, is drawn slowly backward by his gaze and comes in closing the door*) No!

WOMAN. (*Moaning*) The path--is so--steep!

HOLGER. (*Goes to her and bends over her*) Didst thou speak, dame? (*The* WOMAN *does not answer*) Thou art like Grandmother, and I know what Mother would do for *her*! (*Feeling her hands*) Art warmer, dame?--still cold!--The covers aren't very thick. (*He looks about the bare room, sees the old shawl hanging from the peg near the fire, takes it down and spreads it over the woman*) Thou must get warm! (*Goes to the fire and builds it higher*)

WOMAN. (*Still wandering in her mind*) Berries,--yes, find berries.

HOLGER. Oh, thou art hungry! (*He turns to the shelf, takes his own untasted bowl of porridge, brings it to her*) Dame, here is food!

WOMAN. (*Rousing*) Food, give it to me, child, I am dying for food!

(HOLGER gives her the porridge and sits down on the floor beside her.)

HOLGER. (*Watching her as she devours the porridge*) **Ah, poor soul!**--Why, thou wert starving!--Na, just see!--Mother says that's what makes my little brother so round and rosy, because he eats so much porridge,--you like it, don't you?

WOMAN. It is life itself! (*Her voice has grown young and strong. Sinks back again as she has eaten it all*) Bless thee, Child!

(HOLGER sets the empty dish aside on the hearth and turns to feel her hands.)

HOLGER. Oh, thou art warm!

WOMAN. Aye, warm! (*In a voice increasingly rich and sweet. At this moment there comes the distant sound of organ music.* HOLGER *straightens suddenly in a listening attitude*) Listen,--is that music?

HOLGER. From the Cathedral!--Aye, it must be,--last summer we could hear it plain, and now with so many thousands there! (*Leaves the woman and stands in the center of the room listening attentively*) It's beginning!--(*Pause*) Everyone is there!

WOMAN. Why are they there.

HOLGER. It's the great service! (*He goes toward the window and stands looking out. He talks on half to her, half to himself*) All the world is there, the village folk, and strangers from afar, great court folk, too,--aye, and the King,--our King! And He will give a gift,--a King's gift! (*She rises erectly and follows him across the room. There is the strength and poise of youth in her walk. The heavy black hood has fallen back revealing a head covering of white linen that suggests a sister of Charity and gives her face a look of austerity and sweetness. She is strong, maternal, beautiful. Intuitively,* HOLGER, *in his disappointment begins to lean upon her sympathy. The music grows a little louder and floats into the room*) Look, dame, you can even see the windows gleam! It is so near! It's all beginning and--I--am not there! (*A sob creeps into his voice*)

WOMAN. Son!

HOLGER. Aye, dame? (*He turns and comes toward her, she seats herself on the stool near the window, reaches out a hand and draws him down beside her*)

WOMAN. Thou, too, wouldst go? (HOLGER, *too moved by her sympathy to speak, nods silently and puts up a hand to hide the trembling of his lips. She slips her hand to his shoulder*) Another time thou'll go!

HOLGER. (*Fighting back his tears*) It'll never be the same again! To-night the Christ comes. Bertel said--"The Christ!"

WOMAN. Nay, son, pray to the Christ-child, pray that He does not pass thee by! (*She sits facing the back wall of the hut.* HOLGER *kneels before her, and drops his head in her lap. She lays her hand gently upon his hair and makes the sign of the cross above him*)

> (As they have been talking together, the fire on the hearth has burned itself out and the shadows in the room have crept forward and closed around them till only a faint outline of **HOLGER** and the WOMAN can be distinguished in the glimmer of moonlight shining

through the window nearby. There is a long pause broken only by the boy's sobbing which gradually sinks to silence. As he prays, a faint light begins to grow behind him. The smoke-grimed back wall of the hut has vanished and in its place appears a vision of the cathedral chancel.--One by one objects emerge from the darkness. The light touches the golden altar, the gleaming appointments upon it, the jewel-like tones of the stained glass window above, and the rich carpet under foot; it shows the marble arches at the sides and shines softly on the robe of the kneeling **PRIEST.** As the dim vision grows to clearness, so the music comes nearer and swells forth softly into the Christmas processional. Unconscious of it all HOLGER ***looks up at the*** WOMAN, ***his face swept with despair***.)

HOLGER. Oh, it's no use! I'd rather be all blind and never see than miss the vision that the Christ will send!

WOMAN. (***Gazing at the vision***) Look, look what comes!

HOLGER. (***Staring at the woman's face illuminated by the light from the chancel***) Dame! (***He turns to see where the light comes from and the vision meets his eye***) Oh-h-h-h! (***He crouches back at the*** WOMAN'S ***feet, held spell-bound by the sight. As the music changes the*** PRIEST ***rises slowly to his feet, faces the congregation and makes a gesture of approach. The voices of the choir join the music, and from the left side of the chancel, people begin to enter carrying their gifts***)

(An imperious looking man, richly dressed in black and gold comes first, bearing a heavy box. He approaches the altar, kneels and puts the chest in the **PRIEST'S** hands, and, that the full value of his gift may be publicly recognised, he throws back the lid, heaping up the gold coin with which the box is filled. The **PRIEST** turns, goes up the steps to the altar and raises the chest as high as its weight will permit. The man still kneeling awaits the chimes with superb selfconfidence. The bells do not ring. Slowly the **PRIEST** lowers the gold to the altar, turns, raises his hand in blessing and dismissal. The rich man rises, looking bewildered at his failure, crosses to the right and stands near the altar as the pageant moves on.)

(*The* PRIEST *turns to the next comer*, A COURTIER brave in green and gold, who enters with an air of great elegance, bearing daintily a gilded jewel casket. He kneels, lays it in the **PRIEST'S** hands. The latter turns to go but the **COURTIER** detains him a second, raises the lid of the box and holds up string after string of rich gems. The **PRIEST** carries the jewels to the altar and offers them. The bells do not ring. The **PRIEST** dismisses the **COURTIER,** and the young man rises, turns back with assumed lightness of manner and stands at the left of the chancel, watching with great interest.)

(***A beautiful*** WOMAN clad in flame colored velvet sweeps proudly up to the steps of the altar, kneels, takes from her neck a long strand of pearls and offers it to the **PRIEST.** The **PRIEST** receives the necklace, ascends to the altar and offers the jewels. The woman smiling listens tensely for the chimes. They do not ring. The smile fades as the **PRIEST** turns and blesses her. She rises trying to hide her chagrin in a look of great hauteur, crosses to the right and stands near the man in black and gold with whom she exchanges disdainful smiles over the next arrival.)

(An old white haired man clad in a scholar's robes totters on, bearing with difficulty a large vellum bound book. The PRIEST takes a step forward to relieve the Old Man of his burden, and as he goes up the altar steps the Sage sinks exhausted to his knees, listening with straining senses for the bells.--They do not ring.

The *PRIEST* blesses the old man and helps him to rise. He turns back and stands near the *COURTIER* at the left.)

(A lovely young girl enters, dressed in pale green satin, her arms filled with a sheaf of white lilies. The very way she carries them and bends her head to catch their fragrance shows that to her they are the most beautiful things in the world. Kneeling she gives them into the hands of the *PRIEST,* and as he offers them, she listens with childish confidence for the ringing of the bells.--Still there is no sound save the organ music and the singing of the choir, subdued almost to a breath as the gifts are offered. Abashed as the PRIEST blesses and dismisses her, the young girl steps back and stands near the old Sage.)

(*There is a stir in the chancel, even the* PRIEST turning to watch. The *KING* enters. He is a man of forty with tall distinguished figure and a proud face. His purple robes, richly jeweled, trail far behind him and on his head he wears his crown. Everyone leans forward watching with the greatest tension. The KING, exalted with his mood of selfsacrifice kneels, removes his crown and lays it in the hands of the *PRIEST. HOLGER* crouching in the shadow quivers with anticipation. Again the pantomime of hope and failure. The *PRIEST* turns back to the *KING* and raises his arm in the customary gesture. The *KING* starts to rise then suddenly as though overcome at this spiritual defeat sinks again to his knees before the altar and buries his face in his hands, praying. The *PRIEST* stands with arms crossed upon his breast, regarding him sorrowfully.)

HOLGER. (*Overwhelmed with disappointment, softly to the woman*) Perhaps there are no chimes, perhaps the Christ hears us not!

WOMAN. Have faith,--have faith in God.

HOLGER. I would that I could give my pennies to the Child.

>(*The* KING rises from his prayer and goes sadly to the right, standing near the lady in red.)

WOMAN. (*In a low ringing voice that thrills like the call of a trumpet*) Go up, my son,--fear not--The Christ-Child waits for all!

>(HOLGER breathless with the adventure rises and goes timidly forward out of the gloom of the hut into the splendor of the chancel, looking very small and poorly dressed beside all the great ones. He holds out his pennies to the **PRIEST** who bends and takes them with a tender little smile, and **HOLGER,** crossing himself, too abashed to stand and wait, shrinks back into the darkness and the sheltering arms of the Woman.)

>(*The* PRIEST goes up the steps of the altar and holds the pennies high above his head in consecrating gesture, and as he does so, the organ music breaks off with an amazed suddenness for from above there comes the far triumphant ringing of the chimes, mingled with ethereal voices singing The Alleluia.)

>(*A wave of awe sweeps over everyone in the chancel and as the* PRIEST wheels and gestures them to their knees, they prostrate themselves quickly. **HOLGER,** too, kneels awe-struck but the woman rises to her full height and stands watching. From this time on, she withdraws gradually into the deeper shadows of the hut and is seen no more.)

>(As they all kneel the Angel enters from the right, ascends the

steps of the altar and stands beside the huddled figure of the PRIEST. As she stands there, a single pencil of light shines down upon her from above, a ray of light so brilliant that everything around seems dull in comparision, and while she gives her message, the light above grows till it floods her hair and garments with a miraculous radiance. The **ANGEL** smiles at **HOLGER** and chants in a lovely voice.)

ANGEL. Verily, verily, I say unto you, it is not gold nor silver nor rich pearls but love and selfsacrifice that please the Lord. The Christ-Child was hungered and you gave him meat,--a stranger and you took Him in.

HOLGER. (*In an awed tone*) But I--I have not seen the Christ-Child.

ANGEL. Inasmuch as you have done it unto one of the least of these His Brethern, you have done it unto Him! (*The ANGEL **stands with one hand uplifted, as the music rises in a great crescendo of triumph**. HOLGER, **quite overcome, drops his face in his hands and as the climax of the singing is reached, the whole tableau is held for a moment, then blotted out in darkness***.)

(There is a pause, then the light on the hearth flares up revealing the boy alone, still on his knees, looking up bewildered at the back wall of the hut, where the vision had been. Swiftly he rises to his feet and turns to face the Woman.)

HOLGER. Dame,--dame!--The Chimes,--the star--did you see? (*She is gone, he stares about him looking for her*) Gone! Gone! (*The music still rings softly*) But the Chimes! (*He turns, runs to the window, and flings open the casement. A soft light, half moonlight, half something more luminous pours in upon him. He speaks in a tone of infinite*

happiness, looking upward**)** The stars!--God's Chimes!

THE CURTAIN FALLS SLOWLY.

APPENDIX.

The following suggestions for a simplified staging of "Why The Chimes Rang" are offered, not to college dramatic societies or other expert amateurs but to the many young people in the secondary schools, Sunday schools and country districts, who would enjoy staging short plays if it could be done without elaborate scenery or lighting equipment and without previous experience in stage management.

Simplicity aided by imagination goes far upon the stage, and it should always be remembered that the real aim is the creation of a given emotion in the minds of the audience rather than the creation of a given thing upon the stage. If a circle of gilt paper on the head of a fine looking lad can create a vivid impression of kingly dignity, all the crown jewels of Europe cannot better the paper for stage purposes.

In producing a play, it should first be carefully read to see what main impression is to be conveyed, and what chief elements are to be emphasized to make up this impression. The details can then be worked out in harmony with the more important factors.

In "Why The Chimes Rang," religious exaltation is the mood to be created, and the divine beauty of charity is the main theme.

Three sharply contrasted effects are called for: the wood-chopper's hut, dark and humble; and, set against this, the earthly splendor of the cathedral chancel, which in its turn is dimmed by the miraculous presence of the angel.

It is expected that this play will be adapted, by those giving it, to the form and degree of ritual desired. Censers and candles may be used or not, altar appointments and priestly vestments may be chosen to suit the taste of those concerned. Indeed, in all respects, a play must be suited to the conditions under which it is presented and the audience before whom it is given; and while the text may not be altered or added to, lines may be omitted if desired.

The information here given has been gathered from frequent working over of the material but at best it can only help in a general way. Any one producing a play must work out his own problems in detail. One of the things that makes the staging of plays such fascinating work is the exercise it affords the imagination in overcoming obstacles.

SCENERY.

For the sake of facing the most difficult form of the problem of amateur staging, let us suppose that this play is to be given in a parlor or hall, without platform, without proscenium arch or curtains, with the walls, floor and ceiling of such material and finish that no nails may be driven into them, and that the depth of the stage is only nine feet. It looks hopeless but it can be done.

Under such conditions the only possible form of scenery is the screen. If the "scenery-man" is a bit of a carpenter, he can build the screens himself, making them as strong and as light as possible, with four leaves a few inches shorter than the height of the room in which they

Why the Chimes Rang: A Play in One Act 33

are to be used, and proportionately wide.--The framework should be braced by cross pieces in the middle of each leaf, and should have stout leather handles nailed to them for convenience in lifting the screen. The right side should be covered with canvas such as is used for scenery, and the screens can then be easily repainted or recovered for later plays.

If it is not possible to have the screens made to order, ordinary Japanese screens may be borrowed or rented, and made to serve as front curtain, and framework for scenery.

Those indicated in the plan as A A and B B serve as the front curtains, the center sections (marked B B) being drawn aside by persons stationed behind them to show the interior of the hut when the play begins. The four screens marked C D and E E form the walls of the hut. In using screens it will be necessary to do without the window and the actual door unless the person in charge of the scenery is clever enough to paint in a window on one panel of the screen and make a door in another. If not, turn the end panel of the screen marked C to run at right angles with the other part, giving the impression of a passage with an imagined door at the unseen end, and wherever in the business of the parts, the children are said to look out of the window, let them instead look down this passage, as though they were looking through the open doorway.

On the right side of the room in the screen marked D, a fire-place may be constructed by cutting away a portion of the screen to suggest the line of the fire-place, putting back of this opening a box painted black inside to represent the blackened chimney, and finishing with a rough mantel stained brown to match the wall tint. Of course if the screens are borrowed the fire-place will have to be dispensed with.

At the moment when the vision of the cathedral is to appear, the screens marked E E are parted and folded back disclosing the chancel. Perhaps some church nearby has stored in its basement an old stained glass window, which may be borrowed and used as background for the church scene. Such a window was used in a performance of "Much Ado About Nothing" given some years ago at one of the Eastern colleges. It was dimly lit from behind by electric globes and proved very successful in creating a churchly atmosphere. If this can not be done, cover two of the tallest possible screens with any rich sombre colored drapery and stand them against the back wall. In the Los Angeles production, the chancel was represented by a curtain of black velvet, flanked by two silver pillars, between them the altar. Black makes an exceedingly rich and effective foil for bright colored costumes. Whatever is used for backing in the chancel can be masked if unsatisfactory by Christmas greens, which should be arranged in long vertical lines that carry the eye up as high as possible and give a sense of dignity, or in the Gothic curves suggestive of church architecture.

Against this background, and in the center of the space, place the altar. This can be made of a packing box painted gold or covered with suitable hangings. In one performance of this play a sectional bookcase which stood in the room was hung with purple cheese cloth and served as an altar. Should the stage space be deep enough broad steps before the shrine will give an added height to the priest and the angel.

If it is possible to have real scenery the most illusive method of revealing and hiding the chancel is to have the back of the hut painted on a gauze drop, which is backed by a black curtain. At the cue for showing the chancel the lights in front of the gauze go out leaving the stage dark, then the black opaque curtain is rolled up or drawn aside and as the light is slowly turned on the chancel, the vision begins to take form through the gauze, the latter becoming invisible and transparent when there is no light in front of it. The gauze prevents Holger from actually placing the pennies in the priest's hand but if the two approach the gauze as though it were not there, and stretch out their hands so that they seem to touch, the priest being provided with additional pennies which he holds up at the altar, no one in the audience would guess that the coins had not been given him by the child.

Very few halls ostensibly built to house amateur play-giving are adequate for the purpose.--Often the stage is merely a shallow platform without curtains to separate the actors from the audience, and the ceiling and walls surrounding the stage are so finished that the necessary screws for hanging curtains, may not be driven into them. The amateur manager reaches the depths of despair when he finds that even the floor of the shallow platform offered him, is of polished hardwood and may not be marred by the screws of stage braces.

Amateurs who have any voice in the preparation of the stage being built for them, should urge the following specifications:

1. The ceiling of the stage to be at least twice as high as the proscenium arch.

2. The depth of the stage to be at least fifteen feet, deeper if the size of the place permits.

3. The flooring, walls and ceiling of the stage to be of soft wood, into which nails and screws may be driven; or if the main construction is of brick, concrete or metal, some inner wooden scaffolding or other overhead rigging capable of supporting scenery should be provided.

4. There should be some space on both sides of the stage for keeping scenery and properties to be used later in the play, and as a waiting place for actors temporarily off the stage. The platform forming the stage proper should be continued over these wings so that actors leaving the scene may walk off on a level and not seem to plunge cellarward in making their exits.

LIGHTING.

The important thing to be remembered about the lighting is the crescendo of light which occurs as the play runs its course. First the dim little hut so lit by the firelight, that the expressions on the faces of the actors can just be seen without straining the eyes of the audience. Then the rich but subdued lighting of the chancel and finally the brilliant radiance shining on the angel.

Experiments with electricity should not be attempted by persons who do not understand its use, but if there is a competent electrician in the group putting on the play, use electric lighting by all means. No other form of light is so easily controlled or begins to give such effects for stage purposes.

The problems of theater lighting differ with each set of conditions and the best results can only be obtained by actual experiment with the means at hand. Do not feel that because you are an amateur, working with limited equipment, real beauty is beyond you. I have seen a stage picture approaching a Rembrandt in its charm of coloring and skilful use of shadows, created on a tiny stage with few appliances by an amateur who understood his lights.

If electricity is to be had, use three or four incandescent globes for the fire on the hearth, arranging logs of wood around them to simulate a fire. Additional lights as needed can be placed at the side off stage, or in the footlights; or better, if the stage has a real proscenium these supplementary lights can be put in a "trough" that protects and intensifies them and hung overhead in the center against the back of the proscenium arch.

As all these lights are to give a firelight effect, the incandescent globes should be dipped in a rich amber shade of coloring medium which may be bought at any electrical supply house for sixty cents per half pint. If gas or oil is used a firelight effect can be obtained by slipping amber gelatine screens in front of the lamps. These "gelatines" are about two feet square and cost only ten cents apiece.

If the fire-place cannot be made, then a charcoal brazier will serve as an excuse for light and give a sense of warmth to the scene. The brazier can easily be made by any tinsmith from a piece of sheet iron supported on three legs, and there is an illustration of it in the right hand corner of the accompanying scenery plate.--An electric torch or even an ordinary lantern can be slipped inside the little stove to give out a faint glow. A piece of one of the amber screens put over the torch or lantern will warm the light and the brazier can be placed anywhere in the hut.

The chancel may be lighted by a number of incandescent bulbs hidden at the sides of the scene, with the light so shielded that it shines on the altar and not into the hut. An especially effective place to put a strong light is inside the box representing the altar, with a hole cut in the top of the box so that the light shines up, giving a central radiance to the appointments of the altar and throwing into prominence the face and costume of each person who approaches it. If any of this light seems glaring it can be softened and diffused by masking it with amber or straw colored cheesecloth.

Some form of search light is practically a necessity for producing the heavenly radiance that shines upon the angel. If procurable, a "baby spot light" is the best appliance, but lacking this, an automobile lamp and its battery can be used.

It is important that all light in the hut should go out when the vision of the chancel appears so that the hut becomes merely an inner proscenium or dark frame around the rich picture of the altar. This of course does not mean that the lantern in the brazier need be extinguished as the light given by that is negligible.

After the angel ceases speaking the tableau of the altar scene should be held as the music grows louder and louder through the final crescendo; then, when the final note has been sung, blot out the stage by extinguishing all lights. Give a moment of darkness during which the back wall of the hut is replaced, and the old woman slips out of the nearest opening in the scenery. Then turn on the front lights which illuminated the hut during the first part of the play.

MUSIC.

The three pieces of music required for this play are as follows:

"The Sleep of the Child Jesus" part song for mixed voices by F.A. Gevaert.

Eightfold Alleluia composed for "Why the Chimes rang" by Percy Lee Atherton.

These two pieces come published together in a special edition for use with this play by The Boston Music Company. Price 15 cents per copy, postpaid.

The bell movement (in five flats) (Postlude) by J. Guy Ropartz. Published by The Boston Music Company. Price 30 cents per copy, postpaid.

For all the music, address The Boston Music Company, 116 Boylston Street, Boston, Mass.

The pieces by Ropartz and Gevaert were chosen for the Workshop production by Dr. A.T. Davison, organist at Appleton Chapel, Harvard University, and are admirably fitted to the play. Mr. Atherton's Alleluia is also just what is needed, both in length and in the triumphant crescendo which carries the piece fittingly and dramatically to its close. It would be difficult to replace this finale except by other music written for the purpose.

The music is perhaps the most important single element in the play. In the original version the scene in the chancel was carried by dialogue but production showed the mistake. From the time that the music begins, it, with the pantomimic action of the actors is all sufficient to interpret the mood and meaning of the scene.

A small parlor organ is practically a necessity and can probably be procured for the cost of the cartage.

A choir of men's and women's voices is best for the singing but a good quartette will serve.

For the bells, the long tubular chimes which are suspended by one end and struck with a wooden hammer are the most satisfactory. If they seem too metallic, try covering the head of the hammer with folds of chamois skin. If such a set of chimes is not to be had a substitute can be found in the phonograph, for which there are a number of chimes records.--The tune played on the phonograph must not be a modern one; Luther's Hymn "Great God, what do I see and hear?" (A Columbia record) is the best. The tune can be disguised by lifting the needle occasionally and setting it down gently on another part of the record. As far as I know, no phonograph record presents chimes pure and simple. It should be remembered however that the phonograph record lacks the vitality of tone and the note of jubilant triumph which a good musician can bring from the bells themselves.

With the exception of the crescendo at the end of the Alleluia, the music is kept soft and dreamy throughout. It is a temptation to try to achieve this effect by placing singers and organ back, off stage, so that the sound may come from a distance but it has been found that the whole performance gains immeasurably if the organist is in front where he can watch every movement of the actors and interpret them in his playing.

The music begins on Holger's speech: "Oh thou art warm" and continues in one form or another throughout the play.--The organist commences in the middle of the Ropartz "Sortie," at the top of page 6 and continues this until the back of the hut is withdrawn when he drifts into the accompaniment of the Gevaert song, and plays it through once without the voices. As Holger cries "Dame!"--and sinks back against the woman's knee, this verse should end, and the voices of the choir take up the song with the organ.

From this point on every movement in the chancel is paced to the rhythm of the music. It has been found that a verse of the Gevaert song is just long enough to fit the following action.

A person in the procession enters the chancel, walks to the center before the altar, kneels and presents his gift to the priest. The priest accepts the gift, turns, goes up the steps to the altar, and raises the offering high above his head holding it there a moment waiting for the chimes to ring, then brings his arms down, lays the gift on the altar, turns back to the kneeling figure, and raises his hand in blessing. The person then rises, and steps back to his appointed place to the left or right of the altar, coming to a standstill just as the music ends. As the next verse begins, the next person enters the chancel. The movements should be made with deliberation and dignity and so thoroughly rehearsed that keeping time to the music becomes instinctive, that the actor's mind may be on the expressing of the emotions of assurances that his gift will ring the chimes, and later disappointment that the chimes do not ring.

When it comes Holger's turn to offer the pennies, the music begins again as with the others and accompanies the action through to the moment when the priest holds the pennies high above his head,--here the organ and singing break off abruptly, the chimes ring out and keep pealing for a moment, without other music.

On the first note of the chimes the priest wheels swiftly and with a commanding gesture signals the people grouped about the altar to their knees. He kneels also. The organ begins again, softly playing the final Alleluia. The angel enters from the right side, stands on the step of the altar, the central figure,--all about still kneeling awestruck. As the music continues the angel half sings, half chants the speeches, and underneath her voice, which should be as lovely as possible, come in the voices of the other singers very softly at first, like an echo from afar. As the angel's voice stops, those of the other singers grow into the great triumphant crescendo of the finale. Do not be afraid of holding this tableau while the music finishes.--Indeed none of the chancel scene should be hurried. Take it with great deliberation and give whatever element is holding the scene at the moment, (whether the action or the music) plenty of time to make its effect. The Alleluia is played through twice, once softly during the angel's singing the second time in the triumphant climax. As this second singing ends, the lights on the chancel are blotted out, the back wall of the hut is replaced, the old woman disappears, the lights in the hut go up again revealing Holger standing spellbound staring at the wall where the vision had been. As he turns to speak to the woman and during his final speeches, the organ plays softly as though from a great distance and the chimes ring again but not so loudly as before. This music continues till the front screens are brought together and the play is over.

COSTUMES.

The costumes of this play are mediaeval, picturesque and easily constructed.--The accompanying plates will give the best idea of their general appearance. The amounts of goods required for each are noted below.

First of all, in planning the costuming for a play a definite color scheme should be decided on with due regard for the scenery against which the colors are to stand out and for the lights which will greatly affect all values. Here is an opportunity for delightful study and the exercise of the highest artistic ability. Skilful lighting and a well chosen background will make cheesecloth as effective as cloth of gold. Taste and careful experimentation not money secure the best results.

Family ragbags will often yield excellent material for theatrical costumes, and of much better quality than would be bought new for the purpose. But if the stuff is to be purchased, two materials will be found especially suitable and inexpensive. For the peasants' costumes canton flannel is recommended as it has body and comes in beautiful dark reds, browns and other shades which light up well. For the dresses of the richer group in the chancel, sateen is best. It, too, comes in lovely colors and has a very rich glossy finish, though to give variety an occasional piece of cheap velvet or upholstery brocade is very effective. For trimming these richer garments, bits of fur or passementerie can be used, or the material may be stencilled or even painted freehand. Large gold beads sewed on in a simple design gives the appearance of rich embroidery, as do also flowers cut out of chintz and carefully pasted on.

All of the men's jerkins or tunics are made on the simple lines of a man's shirt, opened a little at the neck and belted in at the waist.

The most inexpensive tights for amateurs are well-fitting cotton underwear, dyed the desired color. The children and Bertel can wear their own plain soft low-heeled slippers. The rich folk in the chancel wear their own slippers and draw on over them, socks dyed to match the tights; these socks if rolled down at the top make a very passable substitute for the Romeo shoe of the period desired.

The following notes refer to the costumes of "Why the Chimes Rang" as shown in the plates, the numbers corresponding to those given the figures therein. The estimates of the amount of goods required are all calculated on the basis of yard wide goods for an adult of average size, except in the case of the two children, the costume of the older being planned for a fourteen year old boy that of the younger for a child of ten.

1. The old Woman: underrobe, cut in straight simple lines, gracefully belted, 5-1/2 yards, cloak and hood, 6 yards. If this cloak is black or nearly so it will help to conceal her entrance and exit, as black against black is practically invisible on the stage.

2. Bertel: jerkin, gaiters and cap (all of same material), 3 yards; shirt, (under jerkin) 2-1/2 yards; cloak, 2-1/2 yards. If preferred Bertel's jerkin can be made with sleeves of the same goods instead of the white shirt showing as in the picture.

3. Holger: jerkin and cap, 1-1/2 yards; cape, 2 yards.

4. Steen: jerkin and cap, 1-1/2 yards; cape, 2 yards.

It may be easier to lengthen the skirts of the boys' jerkins almost to the knee and let them wear regular stockings and bloomers instead of tights. If long sleeves are preferred for them, a pair of stockings cut off at the ankle are easily attached at the arm hole and make very good sleeves.

5. The Angel: outer robe, 7 yards; under robe, 5 yards.

This costume is best made of creamy cheesecloth over an under robe of the same, as cheesecloth is faintly luminous in an intense light. It should be long enough to lie on the floor two or three inches all round as a trailing effect is desirable.

6. Rich Woman: dress, 6 yards.

Her head dress is easily made of stiff white paper rolled up in cornucopia shape and sewed securely, over this a long white veil or scarf is draped.

7. The Rich Man: tunic, 2 yards; shirt, 2-1/2 yards; or 1-1/2 yards if the sleeves and neckpiece can be sewed right into the tunic, doing away with the under garment. If the costumes are to have repeated wear, it will be better to have the shirts made separate and of a washable material, they can then be cleansed more frequently than will be

necessary for the tunics. The Rich Man's chain can be made of the heavy brass chain that comes for draping back curtains.

8. The Priest: under robe, 4-1/2 yards; outer robe 6-1/2 yards. This costume will of course be greatly modified by the custom of the church of which he is supposed to be a representative.

9. The King: tunic, 2 yards; shirt, 2-1/2 yards; robe of office, 4-1/2 yards. The King's tunic in general cut is exactly like that of the other two courtiers (nos. 7 and 12) but handsomer in material and trimming. The robe is just a straight piece that hangs from the shoulder and trails on the ground.

10. Sage: robe, 6 yards.

11. Young Girl: dress, 6 yards.

12. Courtier: tunic, 2 yards; shirt, 2-1/2 yards.

PROPERTIES.

The following list gives the properties needed in the play.--

In the hut:

1. A porridge pot.

2. Three small bowls.

3. Three spoons. If pewter spoons are not to be had, wooden spoons can be bought cheaply.

4. Porridge. Custard or Spanish cream looks like porridge and is more easily eaten on the stage, but hot cream of wheat is also palatable if sweetened and the steam from it will lend a touch of realism to the scene.--It will save time to have it put in the three small bowls before the rise of the curtain, and the bowls can be covered with three little plates to keep the steam in till the food is wanted.

5. Two roughly made but substantial stools, one near the window, the other before the fire. Stools are better than chairs with backs because they do not obstruct the view of the audience during the chancel scene.

6. Three large nails or wooden pegs in the walls strong enough to hold things, one on each side of the fire-place and one near the door. These would be impracticable with scenery made of screens as any weight on the screen would pull it over. A solid wooden chest, as a carpenter's tool chest, could be substituted to hold the children's wraps and the extra shawl for the old woman. The chest could be placed against the screen on the left or right as convenient.

7. Steen's cap and cape.

8. Holger's cap and cape.

9. The extra shawl Holger puts around the old woman.

10. Two bright pennies for Holger's gift.

11. Logs of firewood on the hearth. Not needed of course if the brazier is used instead of the fireplace.

In the chancel:

12. An altar cloth. This is properly a piece of fine linen edged with deep real lace. It should not be so wide as to cover the top of the altar, lest it obscure the light shining up through the hole. It should hang down in front of the altar and at the sides about eighteen inches. A very handsome looking lace altar cloth can be cut from white paper.

13. Candle-sticks.

14. Candles.

15. Two censers: Very passable censers can be made by swinging brass cups on the brass chains that come for looping back curtains.

16. Incense.

17. Charcoal to burn the incense. (This comes in the box with the incense.)

18. Matches to light the incense.

19. The chimes (or the phonograph and record.)

20. The organ.

Gifts to be put on the altar.

21. A chest full of gold coins for the rich man. (This chest should be about six by twelve inches, made of some polished wood. If difficult to find, substitute a money-bag of stout canvas for it.)

22. Gold coin for the rich man. These coins may be made of cardboard

with gold paper pasted over them.

23. A gilded jewel box for the courtier (this can be made from a cardboard box covered with gold paper.)

24. Jewels to fill the gilded box. The smaller things that come for Christmas tree decorations make very acceptable stage jewels.

25. A great book bound in vellum for the sage to give. A heavy book can be covered with wrapping paper the color of vellum.

26. A pearl necklace.

27. A great sheaf of fresh lilies. These can be made at home of tissue paper or very beautiful ones can be bought from the Dennison Manufacturing Company.

28. A golden crown. Made of cardboard coated with gold paper and set with Christmas tree jewels. A more substantial crown can be made of thin sheet brass with all the edges turned like a hem, and trimmed with the inexpensive jewels which come for brass work.

www.bookjungle.com *email: sales@bookjungle.com fax: 630-214-0564 mail: Book Jungle PO Box 2226 Champaign, IL 61825*

The Codes Of Hammurabi And Moses
W. W. Davies

QTY

The discovery of the Hammurabi Code is one of the greatest achievements of archaeology, and is of paramount interest, not only to the student of the Bible, but also to all those interested in ancient history...

Religion **ISBN:** *1-59462-338-4* Pages:132
MSRP *$12.95*

The Theory of Moral Sentiments
Adam Smith

QTY

This work from 1749. contains original theories of conscience amd moral judgment and it is the foundation for systemof morals.

Philosophy **ISBN:** *1-59462-777-0* Pages:536
MSRP *$19.95*

Jessica's First Prayer
Hesba Stretton

QTY

In a screened and secluded corner of one of the many railway-bridges which span the streets of London there could be seen a few years ago, from five o'clock every morning until half past eight, a tidily set-out coffee-stall, consisting of a trestle and board, upon which stood two large tin cans, with a small fire of charcoal burning under each so as to keep the coffee boiling during the early hours of the morning when the work-people were thronging into the city on their way to their daily toil...

Childrens **ISBN:** *1-59462-373-2* Pages:84
MSRP *$9.95*

My Life and Work
Henry Ford

QTY

Henry Ford revolutionized the world with his implementation of mass production for the Model T automobile. Gain valuable business insight into his life and work with his own auto-biography... "We have only started on our development of our country we have not as yet, with all our talk of wonderful progress, done more than scratch the surface. The progress has been wonderful enough but..."

Biographies/ **ISBN:** *1-59462-198-5* Pages:300
MSRP *$21.95*

www.bookjungle.com *email: sales@bookjungle.com fax: 630-214-0564 mail: Book Jungle PO Box 2226 Champaign, IL 61825*

The Art of Cross-Examination
Francis Wellman

QTY

I presume it is the experience of every author, after his first book is published upon an important subject, to be almost overwhelmed with a wealth of ideas and illustrations which could readily have been included in his book, and which to his own mind, at least, seem to make a second edition inevitable. Such certainly was the case with me; and when the first edition had reached its sixth impression in five months, I rejoiced to learn that it seemed to my publishers that the book had met with a sufficiently favorable reception to justify a second and considerably enlarged edition. ...

Reference   ISBN: *1-59462-647-2*   **Pages:412**   *MSRP $19.95*

On the Duty of Civil Disobedience
Henry David Thoreau

QTY

Thoreau wrote his famous essay, On the Duty of Civil Disobedience, as a protest against an unjust but popular war and the immoral but popular institution of slave-owning. He did more than write—he declined to pay his taxes, and was hauled off to gaol in consequence. Who can say how much this refusal of his hastened the end of the war and of slavery?

Law   ISBN: *1-59462-747-9*   **Pages:48**   *MSRP $7.45*

Dream Psychology Psychoanalysis for Beginners
Sigmund Freud

QTY

Sigmund Freud, born Sigismund Schlomo Freud (May 6, 1856 - September 23, 1939), was a Jewish-Austrian neurologist and psychiatrist who co-founded the psychoanalytic school of psychology. Freud is best known for his theories of the unconscious mind, especially involving the mechanism of repression; his redefinition of sexual desire as mobile and directed towards a wide variety of objects; and his therapeutic techniques, especially his understanding of transference in the therapeutic relationship and the presumed value of dreams as sources of insight into unconscious desires.

Psychology   ISBN: *1-59462-905-6*   **Pages:196**   *MSRP $15.45*

The Miracle of Right Thought
Orison Swett Marden

QTY

Believe with all of your heart that you will do what you were made to do. When the mind has once formed the habit of holding cheerful, happy, prosperous pictures, it will not be easy to form the opposite habit. It does not matter how improbable or how far away this realization may see, or how dark the prospects may be, if we visualize them as best we can, as vividly as possible, hold tenaciously to them and vigorously struggle to attain them, they will gradually become actualized, realized in the life. But a desire, a longing without endeavor, a yearning abandoned or held indifferently will vanish without realization.

Self Help   ISBN: *1-59462-644-8*   **Pages:360**   *MSRP $25.45*

www.bookjungle.com *email: sales@bookjungle.com fax: 630-214-0564 mail: Book Jungle PO Box 2226 Champaign, IL 61825*

QTY

- [ ] **The Rosicrucian Cosmo-Conception Mystic Christianity** by *Max Heindel*   ISBN: *1-59462-188-8*   **$38.95**
  The Rosicrucian Cosmo-conception is not dogmatic, neither does it appeal to any other authority than the reason of the student. It is: not controversial, but is: sent forth in the, hope that it may help to clear...   New Age/Religion Pages 646

- [ ] **Abandonment To Divine Providence** by *Jean-Pierre de Caussade*   ISBN: *1-59462-228-0*   **$25.95**
  "The Rev. Jean Pierre de Caussade was one of the most remarkable spiritual writers of the Society of Jesus in France in the 18th Century. His death took place at Toulouse in 1751. His works have gone through many editions and have been republished...   Inspirational/Religion Pages 400

- [ ] **Mental Chemistry** by *Charles Haanel*   ISBN: *1-59462-192-6*   **$23.95**
  Mental Chemistry allows the change of material conditions by combining and appropriately utilizing the power of the mind. Much like applied chemistry creates something new and unique out of careful combinations of chemicals the mastery of mental chemistry...   New Age Pages 354

- [ ] **The Letters of Robert Browning and Elizabeth Barret Barrett 1845-1846 vol II**   ISBN: *1-59462-193-4*   **$35.95**
  by *Robert Browning* and *Elizabeth Barrett*   Biographies Pages 596

- [ ] **Gleanings In Genesis (volume I)** by *Arthur W. Pink*   ISBN: *1-59462-130-6*   **$27.45**
  Appropriately has Genesis been termed "the seed plot of the Bible" for in it we have, in germ form, almost all of the great doctrines which are afterwards fully developed in the books of Scripture which follow...   Religion/Inspirational Pages 420

- [ ] **The Master Key** by *L. W. de Laurence*   ISBN: *1-59462-001-6*   **$30.95**
  In no branch of human knowledge has there been a more lively increase of the spirit of research during the past few years than in the study of Psychology, Concentration and Mental Discipline. The requests for authentic lessons in Thought Control, Mental Discipline and...   New Age/Business Pages 422

- [ ] **The Lesser Key Of Solomon Goetia** by *L. W. de Laurence*   ISBN: *1-59462-092-X*   **$9.95**
  This translation of the first book of the "Lernegton" which is now for the first time made accessible to students of Talismanic Magic was done, after careful collation and edition, from numerous Ancient Manuscripts in Hebrew, Latin, and French...   New Age/Occult Pages 92

- [ ] **Rubaiyat Of Omar Khayyam** by *Edward Fitzgerald*   ISBN:*1-59462-332-5*   **$13.95**
  Edward Fitzgerald, whom the world has already learned, in spite of his own efforts to remain within the shadow of anonymity, to look upon as one of the rarest poets of the century, was born at Bredfield, in Suffolk, on the 31st of March, 1809. He was the third son of John Purcell...   Music Pages 172

- [ ] **Ancient Law** by *Henry Maine*   ISBN: *1-59462-128-4*   **$29.95**
  The chief object of the following pages is to indicate some of the earliest ideas of mankind, as they are reflected in Ancient Law, and to point out the relation of those ideas to modern thought.   Religiom/History Pages 452

- [ ] **Far-Away Stories** by *William J. Locke*   ISBN: *1-59462-129-2*   **$19.45**
  "Good wine needs no bush, but a collection of mixed vintages does. And this book is just such a collection. Some of the stories I do not want to remain buried for ever in the museum files of dead magazine-numbers an author's not unpardonable vanity..."   Fiction Pages 272

- [ ] **Life of David Crockett** by *David Crockett*   ISBN: *1-59462-250-7*   **$27.45**
  "Colonel David Crockett was one of the most remarkable men of the times in which he lived. Born in humble life, but gifted with a strong will, an indomitable courage, and unremitting perseverance...   Biographies/New Age Pages 424

- [ ] **Lip-Reading** by *Edward Nitchie*   ISBN: *1-59462-206-X*   **$25.95**
  Edward B. Nitchie, founder of the New York School for the Hard of Hearing, now the Nitchie School of Lip-Reading, Inc, wrote "LIP-READING Principles and Practice". The development and perfecting of this meritorious work on lip-reading was an undertaking...   How-to Pages 400

- [ ] **A Handbook of Suggestive Therapeutics, Applied Hypnotism, Psychic Science**   ISBN: *1-59462-214-0*   **$24.95**
  by *Henry Munro*   Health/New Age/Health/Self-help Pages 376

- [ ] **A Doll's House: and Two Other Plays** by *Henrik Ibsen*   ISBN: *1-59462-112-8*   **$19.95**
  Henrik Ibsen created this classic when in revolutionary 1848 Rome. Introducing some striking concepts in playwriting for the realist genre, this play has been studied the world over.   Fiction/Classics/Plays 308

- [ ] **The Light of Asia** by *sir Edwin Arnold*   ISBN: *1-59462-204-3*   **$13.95**
  In this poetic masterpiece, Edwin Arnold describes the life and teachings of Buddha. The man who was to become known as Buddha to the world was born as Prince Gautama of India but he rejected the worldly riches and abandoned the reigns of power when...   Religion/History/Biographies Pages 170

- [ ] **The Complete Works of Guy de Maupassant** by *Guy de Maupassant*   ISBN: *1-59462-157-8*   **$16.95**
  "For days and days, nights and nights, I had dreamed of that first kiss which was to consecrate our engagement, and I knew not on what spot I should put my lips..."   Fiction/Classics Pages 210

- [ ] **The Art of Cross-Examination** by *Francis L. Wellman*   ISBN: *1-59462-309-0*   **$26.95**
  Written by a renowned trial lawyer, Wellman imparts his experience and uses case studies to explain how to use psychology to extract desired information through questioning.   How-to/Science/Reference Pages 408

- [ ] **Answered or Unanswered?** by *Louisa Vaughan*   ISBN: *1-59462-248-5*   **$10.95**
  Miracles of Faith in China   Religion Pages 112

- [ ] **The Edinburgh Lectures on Mental Science (1909)** by *Thomas*   ISBN: *1-59462-008-3*   **$11.95**
  This book contains the substance of a course of lectures recently given by the writer in the Queen Street Hail, Edinburgh. Its purpose is to indicate the Natural Principles governing the relation between Mental Action and Material Conditions...   New Age/Psychology Pages 148

- [ ] **Ayesha** by *H. Rider Haggard*   ISBN: *1-59462-301-5*   **$24.95**
  Verily and indeed it is the unexpected that happens! Probably if there was one person upon the earth from whom the Editor of this, and of a certain previous history, did not expect to hear again...   Classics Pages 380

- [ ] **Ayala's Angel** by *Anthony Trollope*   ISBN: *1-59462-352-X*   **$29.95**
  The two girls were both pretty, but Lucy who was twenty-one who supposed to be simple and comparatively unattractive, whereas Ayala was credited, as her Bombwhat romantic name might show, with poetic charm and a taste for romance. Ayala when her father died was nineteen...   Fiction Pages 484

- [ ] **The American Commonwealth** by *James Bryce*   ISBN: *1-59462-286-8*   **$34.45**
  An interpretation of American democratic political theory. It examines political mechanics and society from the perspective of Scotsman James Bryce   Politics Pages 572

- [ ] **Stories of the Pilgrims** by *Margaret P. Pumphrey*   ISBN: *1-59462-116-0*   **$17.95**
  This book explores pilgrims religious oppression in England as well as their escape to Holland and eventual crossing to America on the Mayflower, and their early days in New England...   History Pages 268

www.bookjungle.com email: sales@bookjungle.com fax: 630-214-0564 mail: Book Jungle PO Box 2226 Champaign, IL 61825

QTY

The Fasting Cure *by Sinclair Upton* ISBN: *1-59462-222-1* **$13.95**
In the Cosmopolitan Magazine for May, 1910, and in the Contemporary Review (London) for April, 1910, I published an article dealing with my experiences in fasting. I have written a great many magazine articles, but never one which attracted so much attention... *New Age/Self Help/Health Pages 164*

Hebrew Astrology *by Sepharial* ISBN: *1-59462-308-2* **$13.45**
In these days of advanced thinking it is a matter of common observation that we have left many of the old landmarks behind and that we are now pressing forward to greater heights and to a wider horizon than that which represented the mind-content of our progenitors... *Astrology Pages 144*

Thought Vibration or The Law of Attraction in the Thought World ISBN: *1-59462-127-6* **$12.95**
by William Walker Atkinson *Psychology/Religion Pages 144*

Optimism *by Helen Keller* ISBN: *1-59462-108-X* **$15.95**
Helen Keller was blind, deaf, and mute since 19 months old, yet famously learned how to overcome these handicaps, communicate with the world, and spread her lectures promoting optimism. An inspiring read for everyone... *Biographies/Inspirational Pages 84*

Sara Crewe *by Frances Burnett* ISBN: *1-59462-360-0* **$9.45**
In the first place, Miss Minchin lived in London. Her home was a large, dull, tall one, in a large, dull square, where all the houses were alike, and all the sparrows were alike, and where all the door-knockers made the same heavy sound... *Childrens/Classic Pages 88*

The Autobiography of Benjamin Franklin *by Benjamin Franklin* ISBN: *1-59462-135-7* **$24.95**
The Autobiography of Benjamin Franklin has probably been more extensively read than any other American historical work, and no other book of its kind has had such ups and downs of fortune. Franklin lived for many years in England, where he was agent... *Biographies/History Pages 332*

Name	
Email	
Telephone	
Address	
City, State ZIP	

☐ Credit Card   ☐ Check / Money Order

Credit Card Number	
Expiration Date	
Signature	

Please Mail to: Book Jungle
PO Box 2226
Champaign, IL 61825
or Fax to: 630-214-0564

ORDERING INFORMATION

web: *www.bookjungle.com*
email: *sales@bookjungle.com*
fax: *630-214-0564*
mail: *Book Jungle PO Box 2226 Champaign, IL 61825*
or PayPal *to sales@bookjungle.com*

Please contact us for bulk discounts

DIRECT-ORDER TERMS

20% Discount if You Order Two or More Books
Free Domestic Shipping!
Accepted: Master Card, Visa, Discover, American Express

www.ingramcontent.com/pod-product-compliance
Lightning Source LLC
Chambersburg PA
CBHW081330040426

42453CB00013B/2365